Coming Home

Uncovering the Foundations of Psychological Well-being

Cataloging in Publication

ISBN 13: 978-1532807831

Project Editor: Gary Whyte
Graphic Design: Kontrast – Graphic Design
Cover Photo: Dicken Bettinger
Author Photo: Chris Nunan

Endorsements

In Coming Home, Dr. Bettinger and Mrs. Swerdloff present Sydney Banks' discovery of the Three Universal Principles at the source of creation and all human experience in a way that helps illuminate Syd's profound and universal message of hope. They point with certainty and clarity to the understanding that guides every one of us back home to our natural peace of mind, love, and wisdom. This book has the ability to help you wake up to your innate mental health regardless of your past experiences, past misdeeds, present challenges, or future uncertainties. This extraordinary book deeply touched my heart and soul.

— William F. Pettit Jr., MD, Psychiatrist, Three Principles'
student and sharer

You will come home whilst reading this book. Coming Home is a generous gift that allows us to gently uncover our true, intelligent, and loving natures. I cannot imagine anyone reading Natasha and Dicken's book and not experiencing a shift in mind and soul. The authors take us with them on a journey. It is not only a journey of experiencing the love and wisdom within, but it is a journey of the most important education we could ever receive about the Three Principles that define the inner space that Dicken and Natasha call "home."

— Terry Rubenstein, Director of Innate Health Centre
in London, author of *Exquisite Mind*

The peaceful feeling and quiet whisper of spiritual truth can be found on every page of this wonderful book. The simple principles shared inside will help you find your way back home to the space of pure consciousness within.

— Michael Neill, bestselling author of
The Inside-Out Revolution and *The Space Within*

In gratitude

We are grateful for all that we have learned from our friends, family, students, and teachers throughout the years.

We cannot thank enough our spouses, Coizie and John, for their outpouring of love and support. The ways in which they have encouraged and nourished us, as well as given us feedback and suggestions, have been invaluable. We dedicate this book to them with our deepest gratitude and love.

We are especially grateful for our teacher, Sydney Banks, who had a profound realization of the foundations of human psychological functioning. This realization led to his message of hope: that every human being already has within themselves what they need to live a healthy, loving life. We have both been greatly inspired by his teachings. More than anyone we have met, he has pointed us directly home to our essential nature. He encouraged us to listen for and trust the way in which wisdom reveals itself to us and then guides us through life.

It is our hope that this book will contribute to the spirit of the work started by Mr. Sydney Banks.

We have enjoyed collaborating on this book. Collaboration allowed us to reflect together and continually go deeper so that the material would be fresh and evolving.

It is our heartfelt wish that as you reflect on this book you will realize your true home and will uncover all the love and understanding you need to live a beautiful life.

The beauty of collaboration

We met in May 2014 and immediately recognized each other as kindred spirits. We started having conversations about our understanding of the inside-out nature of life, and soon the conversations turned into long emails where we shared our reflections on the Principles. This sharing was both enriching and inspiring.

Within weeks, and simultaneously, we had the idea of writing a book together. We had each been wanting to write a book, and we both had students and clients asking when a book would come out. Neither of us had ever thought we would write with someone else, but we recognized that wisdom was pointing us toward collaboration.

As we wrote, there were times when one or the other of us would not like how the writing was coming out. When this happened, we pulled back and trusted that wisdom would come up with something that would be fresh and true for us both. When there was a discrepancy between us we became curious to hear what the other person was seeing. Then we became quiet until we came to a new clarity and discovered how to express the idea in a way that made sense to us. Writing together was so much easier because we knew that our comments and feedback to each other would not be seen as personal criticism, but as an invitation to listen deeply and let wisdom weigh in. We have enjoyed this beautiful dance between knowing and not knowing.

Because we live in two different countries, we have written most of the book online via screen sharing on Skype. We have also had the opportunity to meet in USA, England, Finland, and Denmark to work on the structure and format of the book. Each time we have met, the book has become more alive and has evolved in an organic way.

We are so grateful for what we have continued to learn about the Principles. Our understanding has really helped us in our collaborative writing while the process of writing itself has deepened our trust and respect in the power of wisdom. Wisdom continually brought us just the right words as we attempted to express what is deeper than words.

We have experienced for ourselves that, ultimately, collaboration is not just an interaction between two people but is really a listening for a shared wisdom. Our best collaboration happened when our egos were not in the picture and we allowed the creative process to write the book.

Table of Contents

Part 6: Living a life aligned with love and wisdom

Part 7: Realizing the deep quiet of your being

Part 8: Coming home

About the authors

Resources

Welcome

*You already have within you all that you need
for psychological well-being.*

*The capacity for love and understanding
is already complete within you.*

*Deep within, waiting to be uncovered,
is your wisdom. It exists beyond anything that
you are thinking.*

This book is an invitation for you to realize ever more deeply
the infinite potential that is found within. "Within" means beyond
your thinking. This wisdom is untouched by any memory, no matter
how painful that memory may be. This wisdom lies beyond any
experiences you have had or are now having, and is prior to any
beliefs or ideas you have about yourself.

It is our deepest wish that you get a glimpse of, or a sense of,
or a feel for, this inner space to which we are trying to point you.
When you touch this space, you will gently fill with a pleasant feeling
of well-being. This feeling may be as subtle as a sense of being
comfortable with whatever you are feeling. It may be a slight feeling
of relaxation or ease, or it may be an all-encompassing feeling of
peace, joy, or love. It is inevitable that you will feel at ease as a result
of resting in this vast space within. This space is always there when
your personal thinking falls away.

We are using the metaphor of "coming home" for the experience
you have when you rest in this dimension of life.

Home is often a place where we put on our most comfortable clothes, sit in our most comfortable spot, and completely let go and relax. In this context, coming home is a letting go of all pretenses and just being your true self. It is the place inside of you where you feel most at ease.

Perhaps you haven't realized how readily available this dimension is to you in your life.

Our hope is that this essential dimension of home becomes more real to you. As this happens, we know you will be able to bring more love and understanding into your life and into the world.

Discovering your depth

You're not just a physical being. You're something far greater. Go beyond the physical to the spiritual part of you. There you will find more power than you've ever realized in your life.

"The Washington Lectures: Separate Realities"
— Sydney Banks

You can keep discovering a deeper dimension of what it means to be a human being.

Your true nature is pure being — invisible, yet essential. It is full of creative potential. It is formless. It is what many would call spiritual. As you experience and realize this dimension of being, it reveals to you more of your innate psychological well-being. It reveals an inner world of beautiful feelings such as peace, joy, happiness, compassion, and gratitude. It reveals the richness of living fully in the now. It reveals a higher order of thinking with characteristics such as clarity, insight, perspective, motivation, inspiration, creativity, and common sense solutions to your daily challenges.

Awareness of your true nature
awakens well-being.

This awareness enlivens you and allows you to live in a more lighthearted way. It helps you to recognize that you are already deeply connected to others and to life.

In this book, we would like to remind you of this dimension of who you really are. We will be pointing you in a direction that you may not be accustomed to looking. We will be repeating ourselves throughout the book because repetition helps when it comes to gaining insight.

If you listen deeply and are patient, we just know that you will gain greater awareness of this dimension.

When you truly listen and are patient, you will begin to realize something that on the deepest level you recognize is true about you and all humans. You will get a glimpse of the fundamental nature you share with all of your fellow human beings. Each time you get a glimpse of this, it will change your life. It has done so for us and for countless thousands of people all over the world who have taken up this enjoyable exploration.

This is not a "how to" book. In our experience, fundamental change does not require hard work and practice! The essence of transformational change is insight, recognition, or realization.

You, like everyone else, already have everything you need for transformational change.

When your mind is relaxed and open, you are primed to have insights. Insights are just subtle shifts of feeling inside you. With these shifts of feeling, things will look better to you. Things will come easier to you.

You are more likely to experience these internal shifts if you pause and reflect frequently. To reflect means to set aside all attempts on your part to try to figure anything out. We will be pointing you toward an inner dimension that is impossible to understand with your intellect or through analysis. Insights require nothing of your intellect. To reflect is to simply relax and feel for, or sense deeply, the quiet of your mind. The quiet of your mind is the most alive, dynamic, and creative aspect of yourself. For us, and for many others, it is similar to falling asleep.

It is pleasurable to rest in the quiet of your mind.

As you read, listen to where our words are pointing you. As strange as it sounds, don't think about the words. They are just pointers. Listening this way is like listening to your favorite music. It's hard to enjoy music at the same time you are paying attention to, and thinking about, the notes. When enjoying, you are simply letting the music in and absorbing it.

Our words are simply our best attempt to point you toward your essence. We are inviting you to look beyond everything we say. Your essence is beyond all words, ideas, and concepts, to what actually lies outside these. We are not interested in you understanding anything intellectually. We are asking you to join us in rediscovering what is more than can be seen with the eye or heard with the ear.

The feelings of well-being you, and everyone else, are looking for arise from deep within the quiet of your mind. When you stop and reflect, you allow your mind to quiet so you have more access to your feelings of well-being. When reflecting, you stop trying to think about anything and just allow your mind to open to what may occur. It is a relaxing and a letting go that is natural to us because it requires no effort.

*Reflection is a relaxed way you can use
your mind to access higher levels of insight,
feeling, and knowing.*

You let go of everything you think you know, and enter into a
dimension that isn't touched or influenced by your personal thinking.
Thoughts may flow through your mind but you are not listening to
them. You rest in this inner quiet until something that feels fresh,
new, and alive arises within you.

We have found reflecting to be an enjoyable and rewarding
experience.

We hope you do, too.

Part 1:
A breakthrough in
understanding human beings

Humanity is fortunate, indeed, when an individual has a realization that is so profound it not only changes that individual's life, but also has relevance for every human being.

In this part we introduce you to one such individual, Mr. Sydney Banks. After he experienced his realizations, he insisted that what he had realized not be about him personally. He was confident that he had had insights into what was universally true for all human beings and that we should listen with an open mind and find out for ourselves if the Principles help raise our own level of well-being.

You have to go beyond all concepts. And you find it in the stillness of your mind, in the quiet chambers of your mind when you go from the known to the unknown, from the physical to the spiritual ....

When you hear beyond the word, an inner light goes on and it brings out inner knowledge and wisdom, spiritual intelligence, before the contamination of human thought.

"Long Beach Lecture Series: The Great Illusion"
— Sydney Banks

In the beginning

We would like to share with you the realizations of a man named Sydney Banks. Syd, as he liked to be called, was an ordinary man. He had a life changing insight followed by a profound epiphany that not only radically changed his understanding of life, but are relevant for, and give hope to, every single human being.

His realizations are about the essential nature of human beings and how every moment of our psychological experience is created. Syd knew that people could realize this for themselves. He recognized that every insight anyone has about these fundamental forces, or Principles as he liked to call them, would raise their overall level of well-being.

We have experienced the truth of this, both in our own lives and in the lives of countless thousands of people to whom we have presented these fundamental Principles. Now we would like to present them to you, and we will start by telling you Syd's story.

Sydney Banks: A breakthrough in understanding human beings

Syd was born in Scotland, had a ninth-grade education, and was working as a welder in a pulp mill on Vancouver Island in British Columbia. Syd thought of himself as being insecure. He lived with the weight of his insecurity, which led him to be quite serious.

Most of us are familiar with the experience of insecurity. Insecurity is a feeling of uncertainty, doubt, and discomfort. It can be a subtle sense of tension in our bodies: tension in our face, neck, shoulders, or stomach.

We can also experience insecurity as a feeling of stress or upset. It can take many forms such as fear, anger, or unhappiness. Often, if we stop and sense within, we can notice this tension somewhere. It can become such a constant companion that we eventually acclimate to it and no longer pay much attention to it until it becomes very strong in our experience.

Can you imagine what it would be like to have one insight that would relieve you from the burden of your insecurity?

Sydney Banks' First Major Insight: It's All Thought!

In 1973, when Syd was 42 years old, he went to a marriage enrichment workshop. There he met a psychologist who was also attending the workshop. During a break in the workshop, they had a conversation. Syd mentioned how hard this workshop was for him because he felt very insecure. To that the man replied: "Syd, you are not insecure, you just think you are." In that moment Syd had his first powerful realization or insight.

My whole world just exploded in front of me.
It was so simple that it just broke me through into separate realities and it was so devastatingly beautiful that all my problems dropped away. They all started flashing past me as just fantasies because I started to realize that insecurity was thought....
All of a sudden to find out that it's all thought, just thought manifesting into a feeling. That realization was so beautiful that I never slept for three days and three nights.

"The Best of Two Worlds"

In a flash of insight, Syd realized that every bit of his feeling was created from thought. He said he felt like a bomb went off in his head and a lifetime of insecurity lifted from his shoulders. What he realized was that all of his insecurity and unhappiness was just a temporary thought creation.

After this insight, Syd looked around him and saw people everywhere thinking up unhappiness, and innocently not realizing that it was being created from their own thinking! He realized that feelings were not caused by the past, or by circumstances, by other people, or by anything other than thought. He realized that feelings are always and only generated from the power of Thought. And he realized that feelings are created from within, not caused from outside of us.

Syd's experience and insight has relevance to every one of us. In a sense his story is the story of every human being. We all live in our own personal reality that, moment-to-moment, is being created from the power of Thought, and we don't realize it most of the time, if at all.

But like Syd, every one of us has the ability to wake up to the fact that our insecurity is just a temporary Thought-created experience, an illusion.

Insecurity comes and goes as our personal thinking comes and goes. In this sense, our insecurity is just an illusion. It has no enduring substance. It is not a part of us. It is not who we are but is only a temporary construct. Syd saw that all thought content is an "illusion" in the sense that it is not a permanent truth, but only a transitory interpretation.

Syd knew that every one of us is able to realize, or wake up to, the creative power of Thought, be free of its limitations, and return to our well-being.

Sydney Banks' Enlightenment Experience: It's all one!

Not long after his first insight, Syd had a profound epiphany, which was a rare and spontaneous enlightenment experience.

Syd was talking to his wife and his mother-in-law when he felt like he lost all sense of self, of them, of the room, and found himself shrouded in white light. In those few seconds he experienced entering and going through this shimmering light.

From this experience he realized that all of life is pure formless energy manifesting into all that has form. He also realized that all existence is "the same energy whether in form or formless." He realized the great oneness of life. After a few seconds he came back into awareness of his surroundings and was filled with intense feelings of love and understanding stronger than he had ever felt before. The depth of his experience is a very rare occurrence in the history of mankind. He turned around to his wife and his mother-in-law and said:

"I am free! I've come home!"

Based on this enlightenment experience, Syd said:

> But there is a greater secret than (my first insight)
> that it is all thought. (The greater secret is that) you
> can step beyond the five senses, and when you learn to
> step beyond the five senses, then you live a happy,
> contented life. A life full of love, because love is always
> the answer no matter what. Love and understanding,
> together create what you would call a beautiful life.
>
> "The Best of Two Worlds"

Syd here is indicating that every single one of us has the ability to get a glimpse of the inner world that is formless, generative, and infinite.

Syd taught that whenever any of us touch this inner space, it reveals itself to us as love and understanding.

Sydney Banks' teaching: The Three Principles

Syd took what he had realized about the nature of life and began to describe this nature as a trinity. He referred to this trinity as the Principles of Mind, Consciousness, and Thought. What Syd was pointing toward when he talked about Principles were the foundations of all psychological functioning. Here is a short description of the Three Principles:

- The Principle of Mind is the source and intelligence behind all of life, including every psychological system.
- The Principle of Consciousness is that which allows us to be aware of life.
- The Principle of Thought is the force that allows us to think and to experience the full range of our thinking.

These Principles create every moment of our experience and allow us to be aware of them. Syd said that in his enlightenment experience these Principles were revealed to him. Syd knew that he had uncovered the universal common denominators behind the whole spectrum of human psychological experiences.

In this book we will explore how it is that as we realize, or become more aware of, the nature of the Three Principles, our overall level of well-being rises.

Later in the book we will describe the Three Principles in greater depth.

Realizing the Principles is simpler than you think!

Let us say this to you again — it bears repeating — as it's often hard for many of those like us who have been steeped in the world of personal and spiritual growth to hear this:

Becoming more loving and wise is not a matter of development, personal growth, or self-improvement!

It is not a matter of working hard on your self to gradually develop the capacity for love. We will not be teaching you a series of techniques or practices that you will have to do in order to become a better person.

Your essential nature is already one of love and wisdom.

Therefore, it is a matter of realizing, or waking up to, what is already here.

When you wake up in the morning, you didn't have to read a book or practice a technique to wake up. Waking up is natural. You are already built to wake up, to realize, to see beyond what you think you know and discover something totally new.

Such realization is a matter of intuiting, getting a sense of, or having an insight into what lies just a thought away from you at all times.

Intuiting this inner world will deepen what you will come to know as the only constant in this world. Everything in experience comes and goes, but the source of experience doesn't come and go. It's what is always here.

We are capable of having insights into an endless variety of things. Every time something in your life has become truly understood, you have had an insight. Whenever something that was difficult suddenly became easier to you, you have had an insight.

The most direct route to having more love and wisdom in your life is to have an insight into your essential nature as a human being.

Insights into your essential nature reveal
your capacity for love and wisdom.

These insights allow more of the love and wisdom that is built into the very fabric of your being to reveal itself to, and as, you.

So realizing your essential being is simple
if you know where to look.

You have insights into many aspects of life every day. It's natural, it happens spontaneously throughout our lives. Insights come to us effortlessly. So often, when our minds are open and relaxed, something new and fresh comes to us. There is no need to *try* to have insights, they happen naturally. As you read this book, trust that at a certain point something will come to you that is fresh and alive. It will feel right and make sense.

You don't have to work to realize your nature,
your nature will reveal itself to you!

Your essential nature

The wise throughout all the ages have said: "If you want to discover peace of mind and a deeper dimension of life, look within." What we mean by looking within is intuiting your essential nature, realizing the Three Principles.

We are human beings. Being is another word for the formless energy that we are. It's what you are made of, it doesn't go away, and it's not something that has been created. Being is what is creating your human form.

Being is your essential nature.

As you realize your inner being, your personal thinking naturally quiets down, your head clears, and you become more present.

When you are present, a lot of the noise, chatter and busyness of your mind begins to quiet down. You start to relax and become more open to life, and you begin to feel at ease and more connected to the world around you. When your thinking quiets down, you begin to feel more comfortable with whatever you are experiencing and the quality of your thinking improves. You gain more common sense, and you get better ideas.

The field of psychology has often pointed toward a variety of causes for your experiences: your past, biochemistry, personality, other people, your circumstances, even your thought content. They explain that the cause of experience comes from something that has already been created or formed, what we are calling the outside world or the world of form.

What Syd found, and what we are describing throughout this book, is a new understanding of the source of experience. In this understanding, experience isn't created by your past, your biochemistry, your personality, other people, your circumstances, or even your thought content.

Understanding leads you within as you realize that every moment of your experience arises from within. It's not coming from outside of you.

It's a whole new worldview that is not outside in, but inside out.

This is the way it's always worked. It's not a theory. It's not a new idea. It's just the way life is unfolding, that out of nothing everything arises. It's a fertile void, which everything arises in and from. You are part of a perfectly designed system that is generating every moment of your existence.

You use the formless Principles of Mind, Consciousness, and Thought to create every experience you have.

Looking within

It can be difficult talking about our true nature because it is completely invisible. Ultimately, it can't be described in words.

It is only when you break free
of your intellect that the Principles truly
reveal themselves to you.

Most people can intuit that we are connected to something greater, something that connects us all, something deeper than words. When we have moments where we realize the truth of that, it does something for us in a big way. Touching this knowing, even just for a moment, can wake us up and open our hearts. It wouldn't make any sense to talk about this invisible space that connects us unless the realization of this really did something helpful for us.

We want to explore what lies beyond the psychological dimension of experience. This is the quiet of our mind. Many people refer to this as the spiritual dimension of life. The way we are using the word "spiritual" refers to the dimension that lies beyond the form of any experience, even beyond what many call spiritual experiences. We are pointing toward the source of every experience that any human being can have. We want you to sense, or intuit, that place that is much deeper than your intellect.

You may have many ideas about spirituality, and the spiritual dimension of life, but none of these ideas are the source. No one can explain this dimension.

You can only use words as metaphors that refer to, or point in the direction of, this formless source of experience.

This direction has nothing to do with the world of ideas and concepts, and has everything to do with the deep knowing that you, and everyone else, can have about your essential nature. Now let's look at the formless Principles behind all of our experiences.

Part 2:
The Three Principles

The Three Principles — Mind, Consciousness, and Thought — are the fundamental forces responsible for the creation of life and for all of our psychological experiences. They comprise the eternal backdrop behind life. This dimension of life is formless so it doesn't change. It's eternal, it's always there. It is something that we can rely on because it doesn't come and go.

Everything in the physical or psychological world comes, goes, and changes. Your thoughts come and go. Every feeling you have comes and goes. Your perception of life comes and goes. So, you are living in a thought-created world and the content of your experience is something that comes and goes and changes. It arises — and then it disappears. One minute you have one thought, and the next minute another thought, and your experience changes from minute to minute. The instant your thinking changes, your experience changes. The Principles refer to what lies before the comings and goings of your experiences.

An understanding of the Three Principles is a never-ending exploration of the foundational energy behind all of life.

Mind, Consciousness, and Thought are spiritual gifts that enable us to see creation and guide us through life. All three are universal constants that can never change and never be separated.

The Missing Link: Reflections on Philosophy and Spirit
— Sydney Banks

The trinity of the Principles

The Principles of Mind, Consciousness, and Thought that Syd Banks identified are the trinity behind all human psychological experience. Together, these three components are the very roots of all human experience.

The trinity expands our sense of who we think we are. No one can exist without them; they are the necessary components through which we acknowledge life. Without any one of these Three Principles, life would not exist for any human being.

Syd Banks used the word "Principle" to refer to that which is most fundamental in life. The Principles are not theoretical constructs or values or concepts. There is nothing in existence beyond or before these infinite, formless Principles.

We are the trinity of Mind, Consciousness, and Thought in action. We use the power of the Principles to create all of our experiences.

The universal common denominators behind all human beings are that we all have a mind, we all are conscious beings, and we all think. If any one of these fundamental processes is absent you don't have a human being.

In talking about the essential, formless nature of the Three Principles we are pointing toward a human dimension that is beyond the intellect; therefore, it is impossible for the intellect to grasp. A characteristic of the intellect is that it reduces the limitless nature of the Principles to an inherently limited concept or idea.

A trinity fights against our intellect's tendency to reduce vastness to a single constricted view. A trinity expands our understanding beyond the limitations of a single point of view.

Imagine looking into the living room of a house through three different windows on three different sides of the house. From one window you see a sofa, from another window you see a fireplace, and from the third window you see a painting on the wall. All views are directed at the same living room and yet each view expands on and creates a more accurate over-all view.

A trinity makes it more difficult for any of us to become too wedded, conceptually, to any one dimension of the Three Principles. The trinity provides a greatly enriched sense of what is being pointed to!

> Mind, Consciousness, and Thought are the three principles that enable us to acknowledge and respond to existence. They are the basic building blocks, and it is through these three components that all psychological mysteries are unfolded. They are what I call the psychological trinity.
>
> *The Missing Link: Reflections on Philosophy and Spirit*
> — Sydney Banks

Let's look at the Three Principles in more depth.

The Principle of Mind

*Mind is the source and intelligence
behind all of life.*

The Principle of Mind is the formless energy that is responsible for the creation of all of life. It exists completely beyond the world of form. It is the eternal stillness and silence that lies before the movement and noise of created life.

Mind is the essential nature of every one of us. There is nothing beyond Mind. It is the source of everything in the universe. Throughout the ages many words have been used to try to point toward this dimension of life: the unborn, the uncreated, the infinite space out of which everything arises, the divine, the quantum field, the great nothingness, emptiness, the fertile void and other names. Feel free to use any word that you like.

Mind is the intelligence that knows how to create every living system and how to operate those systems. In nature, it guides a flower to open up and turn toward the sun. It knows how to turn sunlight into energy for the flower to grow. It knows how to guide salmon back to their spawning grounds. It guides birds on their annual migration.

Our body is a magnificent example of an intelligent system, which operates from the power of Mind. The intelligence behind life is reflected in the fact that two cells multiply and create a baby, and that every cell in the baby's body knows exactly what to do and how to work in coordination with other cells. It's the miracle of life.

In the same way that Mind creates and operates your physical system, it also creates and operates your psychological system. It is always and endlessly generating new thinking and feeling in your ever-changing experience. Because you have free will, you are able to decide what thoughts you bring to life.

When you look right at the source of what is creating your experience moment to moment, you are really looking into the unknown. You are looking into something that cannot be comprehended by the intellect. You are looking beyond any thought, belief, or content. It's like staring into the sky, looking beyond anything that you can see. There is a quiet in that inner space. It is where we, as human beings, feel most relaxed and comfortable. As you look in this direction you can intuit the vast openness of this space.

There is one Universal Mind, common to all,
and wherever you are, it is always with you, always.

The Missing Link: Reflections on Philosophy and Spirit
— Sydney Banks

The Principle of Consciousness

*Consciousness is that which allows all of us
to be aware of life.*

Behind your thinking is an open space of quiet awareness, or
what we call the Principle of Consciousness. The Principle of
Consciousness is the domain of the human soul. The Latin word
for soul is "anima," which is the root of the word animation. We
can, therefore, say that Consciousness is what animates your thinking
and turns it into your sensory experiences so that you can be aware
of what is created.

The Principle of Consciousness is the eternal backdrop behind all
of life. We are all living within an infinite field of consciousness
rather than consciousness only living within the individual.

Everything in life — every single cell that is created in life — since
it is created out of this infinite field of awareness, has built into it
a degree of awareness. Every cell in the universe responds to heat,
pressure, touch, and gravitational forces.

Consciousness is that which allows every human being to be aware
of life. It brings your senses to life — your seeing, hearing, feeling,
tasting, and touching. It's through your senses that you are able to
be aware of life.

Consciousness takes any thought that is created in your head, and
animates it into existence. If you have a sad thought, Consciousness
will animate that thought into existence and you will feel sad.
If you have a happy thought, Consciousness will animate that
thought and you will feel happy.

Consciousness is what allows you to be aware of the role Thought has in creating all of your experiences. It also allows you to be aware of the role that the intelligence of Mind plays in being able to guide you through life.

Consciousness is the gift of awareness.

The Missing Link: Reflections on Philosophy and Spirit
— Sydney Banks

The Principle of Thought

The Principle of Thought is the power behind life that creates the full range of human experiences.

We live in a world of Thought. There is nothing in our experience, from the moment we are born to the moment we die, that isn't brought to life by the power of Thought. It is formless and infinite.

Thought generates every moment of mental activity, or thinking, that is going on inside your head and inside everyone else's head. It creates all the forms of your mental activity, such as ideas, concepts, beliefs, impressions, images, and intuitions. The Principle of Thought is also the power that creates everything you feel and all of your emotions. You are a thinker with free will so you are free to decide what thoughts to listen to and bring to life. You are free to pay attention to a thought or not. You are free to act on a thought or not.

When we talk about the Principle of Thought, we are not talking about the stream of content that is flowing through your head at any given time — that is your personal thinking. The Principle of Thought is much bigger and deeper than that. It's what allows for the creation of all mental life, everything you think, perceive, and feel. There is nothing before this Principle. It is the unlimited creative potential, or field, from which all experiences arise.

You are, like everyone else, always connected to this field. A metaphor for this is waves on the ocean. Every wave of experience that is created anywhere in the world is created out of the same ocean. Right now Thought is generating the specific feelings, sensations, and perceptions that you are experiencing as you are reading this.

The Principle of Thought is impersonal, whereas your thinking content is personal. Your personal thinking is unique to you just as anyone else's personal thoughts are unique to them. We each have our own concepts, ideas, and underlying belief systems. We sometimes call this your conceptual mind. The Principle of Thought exists before your conceptual mind. Therefore, it is before, or prior to, any thoughts you hear in your head and before every single one of your ideas or beliefs. It lies before every label that you put on any person or thing.

Thought is not reality;
yet it is through Thought that our realities
are created.

The Missing Link: Reflections on Philosophy and Spirit
— Sydney Banks

The Principles:
an expanded view of life

Until very recently, the worldview of psychology has primarily focused only on the physical realm of life. It has focused on the forms of experience: thought content, feeling content, behavioral content. This is a materialistic view of life. This view focuses on the already-created content of experience. The Principles expand your view of psychology to include the formless energy that has the power to create your experience. Many people call the formless dimension of life the spiritual dimension.

The Principles bring the "being" dimension out of the background and into the foreground as the essence of human beings. The Principles invite you to look within, toward the formless source of experience. The Principle of Thought invites you to look toward the fact that your feeling experience is created from inside of you. "Inside" refers to the formless nature of your being, rather than from "outside" of you — that which has already been created. The Principle of Consciousness invites you to look within toward the vast backdrop of awareness. The Principle of Mind invites you to look toward the source and intelligence within that transcends your personal intelligence.

As you begin to realize that you are far more than your ever-changing experience, you begin to become aware of yourself as a vast being of limitless creativity, awareness, and wisdom.

A simple metaphor for the expanded view offered by the Principles is that of a tree with its leaves, branches, and roots.

When you only identify with the materialistic view of yourself, it is as if who you are is only a single leaf on a tree. That would mean that you are only a small, insecure leaf being buffeted by the winds of life. But then, if you were to realize that you are connected to the branch and the branch is connected to the trunk and the trunk is connected to the roots, this would do something special for you. Your insecurities would begin to fall away as you saw that you have deep roots and that you are part of this whole, magnificent system called life.

It is understandable how we all develop a limited view of ourselves. We are born into a world of form. As babies we open our eyes and see objects. At some point we begin to think of ourselves as another object in the world. It makes sense that, at some point, you start to identify who you are with the objective nature of your experience. Your identity becomes "I am my thoughts, my feelings, my behavior, and my body."

Fortunately, you are born with the capacity to realize the illusion that you are separate from the whole of life, and also to realize that you are connected to something greater than yourself. It is built into you to realize your true nature.

Even when you forget or lose sight of your true nature, you still always have the capacity to recognize what is true — that there is no separation.

The beauty of this is that there is nothing you have to do to have connection. Connection is not something you get. You are already connected to the formless energy of life.

When you go deep enough, you discover that you are rooted in the infinite nature of life.

Ego: a confined view of life

You limit yourself when you only identify who you are by the content of your experience. You are limiting your sense of possibilities when you only see yourself through a materialistic lens.

It helps to realize that the ideas you have about yourself are not ultimately true. It is normal for you to have thoughts about yourself both positive and negative. But if you identify with any of these thoughts that you have about yourself, then you don't realize that these thoughts are only partially true, made-up ideas, or interpretations.

When your thoughts become your identity that is called ego. Ego is a case of mistaken identity. You believe that the illusory thoughts that come and go are your true self.

Your true self is the dimension of you
that does not come and go.

When you are identified with ego you believe wholeheartedly that your concepts are true. Remember, as babies you were experiencing life directly. You were experiencing life free of your concepts, ideas, and beliefs. You were experiencing life free of the contamination of your negative conceptual thoughts.

Ego's view of life is a conceptual view of life. Concepts are an interpretation. Any interpretation is partial and arbitrary. You might have the idea "I am a good listener" or "I am not good at singing." Ego does not recognize that these are just made up ideas. An idea represents just one interpretation out of an unlimited number of possibilities. It is just a thought. In and of itself, it is not a given reality. It is an illusory reality that will change the instant it is replaced by another thought.

When you become wedded to this narrow and insubstantial view of your conceptual mind you become positional, believing that your view is the only position or the best position. You stubbornly defend your view as the only right view. You get stuck in this view and become dogmatic and rigid. You become unwilling to change. You become arrogant in asserting that you are right and others are wrong.

Being wedded to ego's worldview is what underlies all personal, political, international, and religious conflicts. It is what leads to war.

> *As you realize the true nature of ego,*
> *you wake up to an expanded view of life.*

Part 3:
Some benefits of realizing the Principles

There are profound benefits to realizing the Principles of Mind, Consciousness, and Thought. Over the years we have seen how realizing these Principles has helped relieve emotional suffering in thousands of people.

*The principles can lead you to discover
more beauty and depth of life.*

We have seen wonderful benefits in our clients and in ourselves. We want to give you a sense of how this understanding can be of help to you on a practical, day-to-day level. It may only take one insight to bring enormous benefits to your life.

These benefits are not meant to limit or direct what kind of insights you may have. Wisdom will bring you the insights that are most helpful to you given who you are and what you are dealing with.

You have to go beyond all concepts and you
find it in the stillness of your mind, in the quiet chambers
of your mind, when you go from the known to the
unknown, from the physical to the spiritual. When you hear
beyond the word, an inner light goes on and it brings out
inner knowledge, wisdom, spiritual intelligence,
before the contamination of human thought.

"Long Beach Lectures Series: The Great Illusion"
— Sydney Banks

Personal accountability and the end of blame

How you use the power of Thought determines the experience you will have. This allows you to take full responsibility for your experiences. You begin to see, over and over, "It's all Thought!" and "This feeling I am now having is coming from the use of Thought and nowhere else."

In any moment when you realize that your experience is being created from your use of Thought, you won't be blaming anything or anyone else for creating your feelings. You are using the power of Thought to create your own experience. Yet you probably have heard yourself or others making statements like, "You make me angry," "I am so irritated by this traffic," "My kids are driving me crazy," "I am sad because someone left me," "I am happy because the sun came out," "I am stressed because of all the work I have to do," and on and on.

Realizing Thought keeps you from believing that anything other than Thought is creating your stress. You stop blaming other people for your discomfort or upset. You stop believing that the weather can determine the way you feel, or that someone can make you feel good or bad. You stop blaming the world for your experience. You realize that, in actual fact, it always only works from the inside out.

Whatever you are feeling is always and only determined by how you use the Principles. You no longer feel like a victim of circumstance or people. You no longer feel so insecure, vulnerable, and defensive. You feel secure because you no longer misunderstand where your feelings are coming from.

Becoming more resilient and having less stress

When you recognize that you are the thinker using the power of Thought to shape and determine your psychological experience, you begin to realize that a lot of your thinking is just keeping alive your uncomfortable and tense feelings. You may wonder why you keep engaging in, or holding onto, this thinking if you are the one who has to suffer the results. It is like when you realize that having your hand on a hot stove is what is causing your pain, so you pull your hand away.

Thought recognition naturally allows these thoughts to fall away, or it naturally allows you to stop holding these thoughts to be true. When you stop thinking in a way that keeps your stress and upset alive, your head clears of these upsetting thoughts, and you bounce back to more peaceful states of mind. You get over your tension or your upset more quickly.

As your understanding of Thought deepens, you begin to have fewer stressful responses. You become more immune to stress. The combination of having more bounce and being more immune leads to a greater degree of resilience. Resilience is one of the most important factors of psychological well-being.

More time spent being fully present

Awareness of Thought frees you of the notion that the external world is connected to, and responsible for, creating your feelings. This frees your mind from a lot of unnecessary thinking about the external world. You no longer have to think about what you imagine has caused you to feel the way you do. You no longer have to think about how to change the external world so that you can feel better.

The more aware you are of your connection to the intelligence of Mind, the more you see the benefits of having a quiet, receptive mind. As you come to have less thinking, you naturally become more fully present to life. It is in the present moment that you are able to experience the richness of life.

Greater ease with your inevitable ups and downs

When you wake up to the power of Thought rather than being immersed in the content of your thinking, it brings you into the now. When you are in the now, you still have a flow of thinking coming through you that creates your ups and downs. These ups and downs are normal for all of us to have. But when you don't manage your experience, you have more ease with whatever you are experiencing. It can come and go naturally. You are no longer judging or analyzing your experience, it just flows through without resistance or the need to change or improve your experience. This is accepting what is *as* it is.

Freedom from perceived limitations

As you realize the Principles, you start to see that whatever you are feeling is coming from Thought constructs that are temporary creations. They are illusions, momentary interpretations, ideas, beliefs, and concepts.

Thoughts and feelings come and go. Your perception of life comes and goes. So, you are living in a Thought-created world and the content of your experience is something that comes and goes and changes. It arises, and then it disappears. Just like when you wake up from a dream and realize it was just a dream, you can wake up from your thought "daydreams" and realize they are just momentary constructs or illusions.

Because your thoughts and feelings disappear, they have no substance and therefore they are momentary illusions. It is the power of the Principles that makes them seem so very real to you.

When you are not caught up in your personal thinking, you stop being so influenced by your limiting beliefs. You become free of the limitations of your judgments, your criticisms, your can'ts, your shoulds, your have-tos, your labels, and your beliefs of what is or isn't possible for you to do. You become open to all that is possible.

Forgiveness

Most people think of forgiveness as forgiving someone else's behavior. Let's look at forgiveness from the perspective of the Principles. It is normal to have judgmental thoughts. Judgmental thoughts are thoughts that lower your spirits. Everyone has them. But if you hold onto a judgmental thought, the question becomes, who suffers? Letting go of judgmental thoughts is one way of talking about forgiveness. When you let go of judgmental thinking your spirits lift and you see life with more understanding and compassion.

As you have fewer personal, judgmental thoughts you will be able to more fully experience the richness of each moment. Even in the most ordinary of moments you will feel alive and connected to life itself. You will feel a natural enthusiasm for life. Enjoyment and forgiveness arise naturally from a deeper understanding.

Here is another way you can look at forgiveness. As your understanding of the Principles rises, you realize that each one of us is doing the best we can, given the level of understanding we are in and the thoughts that we think are true. When you see others acting from a low level you can realize that they are, as Syd Banks would say, psychologically "innocent." This does not condone or excuse their behavior but it allows you to realize that we all lose our way. When you lose your way you are caught up in low quality thinking, are taking this thinking to be true, and then are acting on that thinking. When you learn to see the psychological innocence of people you will be less and less affected by their actions.

You can also learn to forgive yourself by seeing your own innocence. When you see your own innocence you are less inclined to hold onto any judgmental thoughts about yourself. This helps you to be more accepting of yourself. When you are more accepting of your own frailties, you become more accepting of the frailties of others.

Forgiveness wakes you up out of your personal thought world and reveals a world of understanding and compassion. Forgiveness allows you to continue to clear away the painful memories of the past that are clogging your mind so that wisdom can break through and guide you toward getting on well with your life.

Forgiveness allows you to be fully restored as a person full of love and wisdom.

More feelings of well-being

Realization of the Principles leads us to a mind that is present and alert, free of the distortions of our conceptual mind. In a free and clear mind we will naturally begin to feel better and lighter. Feelings such as contentment, peace, relaxation, aliveness, happiness, enthusiasm, curiosity, motivation, and love arise in human consciousness when our heads are open and clear. These feelings are like a beach ball underwater — they are always wanting to rise to the surface when they can.

More common sense

There is the thinking that you *do*, and the thinking that *comes to you* when your head is clear. The thinking that comes to you is of a higher order; it helps you through life, guiding you in a healthy direction. A deeper understanding of the Principles brings more clarity, fresh thinking, certainty, and creativity in your thinking. These insights are ordinary, everyday occurrences. They guide you toward common sense responses to your circumstances and challenges.

Benefits to relationships

As you realize your essential nature, your overall level of well-being rises. When this happens, you have more to bring to your relationships. Having insights into the nature of the Principles, and gaining greater understanding and compassion is how any relationship improves.

You live within your unique thought system. You will always see and feel life differently than anybody else. Most arguments between you and others happen when each person assumes that their way of seeing an issue is the right or only way. As you realize the Principles, you become more accepting of the fact that others will always see and feel life differently. Understanding separate realities can make you curious to learn how others are seeing things, without making them wrong.

It will also help your relationships enormously when you realize that your insecurity, stress, or upset feelings are not coming from other people. You will tend to get over your upset feelings more quickly. This allows you to become present sooner and to really listen to the others' point of view.

The insight that nothing the other person says or does is causing you to feel the way you do then generalizes into all your relationships. When blame is not part of your relationships, it becomes easier for you to return to feelings of warmth and caring and common sense that help move the relationship forward.

No matter how bad you feel in your relationships, you can remain hopeful because you are always just a thought away from feeling better. You start to trust that you are never stuck forever in any feeling you may have.

The more you realize the Principle nature of your life, the more well-being infuses your relationships.

Part 4:
Living in harmony with the Principles

Now that we have talked about the Principles and some of the benefits of realizing them, we would like to share with you some of our insights of what it means to live in harmony with them.

This part of the book is our sense of what this means. You can live in harmony with the Principles. The Principles are gifts that you can use wisely. When living in harmony, you get out of your own way. You stop trying to fight against, interfere with, control, or judge your experience in ways that work against you. This allows you to have a greater sense of well-being.

Living in harmony with life is not a process of you doing something.

Harmony arises naturally as you gain a deeper understanding of the Principles. With a deeper understanding, you automatically gain greater well-being.

We describe this process as waking up to the power of Thought, resting in pure Consciousness, and filling with Mind's love and wisdom.

All humans have the inner ability to synchronize their personal mind with their impersonal mind to bring harmony into their lives."

The Missing Link: Reflections on Philosophy and Spirit
— Sydney Banks

Waking up to the power of Thought

By now we hope you are getting the sense that you are living in an ever- shifting, ever-changing Thought-created reality.

There is nothing solid or permanent in your thinking. Every thought you have comes and then it goes. The instant you have a new thought, the last thought you had no longer exists. This is the illusory nature of your thinking. You already have, built into you, everything you need to recognize the nature of this ever-shifting creative process.

You can realize the illusory nature of thought. You can realize that every thought that is created is not true in and of itself. Every thought is neutral. It is a temporary condensation of energy that doesn't mean anything unless you believe it to be true and ascribe meaning to it.

You may have thought "I am stupid," but that thought is not truth. It is only a made-up interpretation. It is "just" a thought. It is not reality; it is only a construct. It is just energy. It is like a cloud that appears and then disappears in the sky. It is like smoke that dissolves into thin air. It is like a mirage that appears real until you look at it from up close and you see that there is no real substance to it. It is like a rope that you, for a moment, believed was a snake. The "snake" is just an illusion.

Just for a moment, consider what it would be like if you realized not a single thought that you had was true. In that moment you would be completely free of the influence of any concepts that were created in your head. You would be free of the apparent truth of your judgments, your doubts, your worries, your self-limiting thoughts, and your "shoulds."

This is what Syd Banks called "the state of no-thought," a state of pure awareness "free of the contamination of your conceptual mind." In this state, you would wake up out of the illusion of thought into the eternal now. You would be free of your conceptual, ego-bound mind. Free of concepts. There is no inside and no outside. What is just is.

You *have* the ability to wake up from the illusion of your personal thoughts, and to realize the true nature of Thought. Then you don't have to be afraid of your thoughts and feelings, you don't have to try to drop your thinking, or get rid of it, or get away from it.

> *Your psychological suffering is simply a function of mistaking your own thought content for truth.*

Every feeling is *always* created from Thought. Every feeling is *only* created from Thought. When you wake up to this fact, you realize the true source of your feelings. Feelings can then serve to point you back toward the source.

When you feel any degree of sadness, anger or fear, such feelings are like an alarm clock waking you up to the power of Thought. Feelings can then serve to point you to your true self — the formless, spiritual dimension of your being.

It truly is like waking up from a dream. When you wake up from a nightmare, you are relieved that it is over. It was just a dream. You have woken up from the apparent reality of what you had been thinking while you were asleep.

In the same way, when you wake up from a "daymare" of insecure thoughts, stressful thoughts, or upset thoughts, you can experience relief that they are just made-up thought constructs and not reality. Your experience of life is not set in stone. Your experiences are like clouds that come and go. You no longer have to believe your daymare. You wake up to a reality free of the limitation of these thoughts.

It can be very helpful for you to wake up out of what might be called negative or self-limiting thinking. You may think, for example: "I am insecure," "I am not lovable," "I am a failure," "I am not worthy," or "I'm not good at...." Or you might think: "I know...," "I am right," "I am better than you," "I am more spiritual than you," or "I am great at...." If you identify with these thoughts as being true of you, then you don't realize they are just made-up ideas and interpretations. It's just thought.

Psychological suffering derives from the belief that a negative or self-limiting thought is true. At any moment, you can be living from a self-limiting conceptual view. It is simply a moment when you have lost sight of the invisible and essential dimension of life.

It is the most natural thing in the world to lose sight of this dimension. When you are born, you experience life directly rather than through the filter of your conceptual mind. After all, you are born into a physical world, have a physical body, and your senses allow you to see objects all around you. Then, as your conceptual mind develops you focus on and think about objects. As time goes on you become more and more identified with your thinking, concepts, and ideas. You start to believe, wholeheartedly, that your concepts are true.

Concepts are an interpretation. Any interpretation is partial, and therefore limited or distorted. Any concept taken to be ultimately true brings you out of harmony with life.

The conceptual mind is not the problem. It's when you become wedded to the narrow, limited views of your conceptual mind that you suffer.

Waking up to Thought frees you from the limitations of your conceptual mind. Paradoxically, it also allows you to use your conceptual mind more wisely.

Free of limiting concepts, your mind is open to experience life directly. You are able to see with fresh eyes and be in harmony with life.

Resting in pure Consciousness

When you wake up from the illusion of your personal thoughts, you wake up from everything you have been thinking. You step back from your personal thinking and, as it quiets down, you become present. You enter into the now, into pure Consciousness — free of the distortions, the limitations, and the contamination of your personal thinking.

In that state, you rest in a space that is before all of your concepts of time. This is why it is often called the eternal now. The now is not *in* time. Time is a concept, and when your mind is free of concepts you find yourself in the timeless now. You are not holding onto any concepts of past, present, or future.

If you are free of concepts of time, you are beyond your ideas of wanting or desiring something in the future. A mind free of wanting and desiring is a mind at peace.

Words such as quiet, silence, or stillness are used to describe this space before the noise, the busyness, the chatter, and the babble of your personal thinking.

When you touch this infinite space your mind is at rest. It is peaceful and calm. There is true contentment.

This space is the deepest essence
of yourself that you can sense.
It is your soul.

Pure Consciousness can also be called the meditative state. This state is not a doing or technique. It is your natural state of mind, free of your personal thinking. Realizing this allows you to relax into yourself as you are. Your natural meditative state of mind is relaxed, open, and alert.

When you rest in this space, you may still have thought content passing through your mind but these thoughts are not paid attention to or listened to. It may feel like you are the sky and your thoughts are birds flying through. Your inner sky is untouched by these birds.

You see life directly, unfiltered by the distortions of your personal beliefs. You see life as it is, rather than as it isn't.

It is a space within and beyond the personal, yet it is something that you already have and are. It is your true self. Some call it the impersonal self.

The more you touch this infinite, wide-open space, the more you realize the fact of its ever-present nature. It becomes more and more real to you. It becomes more and more familiar. It is a space where you can experience directly your true nature. It is the space where you feel most at home.

When you rest in pure Consciousness you are able to simply *be*. This resting is not a doing but a being. It's the most natural position you can be in. It's coming home.

Resting in pure Consciousness allows you
to experience a deeper sense of living
in harmony with life.

Filling with Mind's love and wisdom

Mind is the formless intelligence behind all of life. We are all connected to this universal intelligence. In humans, this formless universal intelligence is often called wisdom.

When you wake up to Thought, and rest in the space of pure Consciousness, you quite naturally and spontaneously fill with thoughts and feelings of well-being. These thoughts and feelings are uplifting; they connect you to life in a positive way and guide you in a healthy direction.

As we have mentioned, realization of Thought wakes you up, out of your conceptual mind and into the now. As your mind opens up and limiting thoughts drop away, you naturally begin to feel more relaxed and expansive. This is how wisdom reveals itself to you as deeper feelings.

Wisdom is contained within these feelings and is not something that you can figure out with your intellect.

Wisdom is contained within the
beautiful feelings that come from the quiet
of your mind.

When you are not in your conceptual mind, words are not needed to describe these feelings of well-being. You can sense, without words, that these feelings are experienced as uplifting, refreshing, and nourishing. This is what everyone is looking for. What a great discovery to find out you can trust that feelings of well-being will come naturally and spontaneously from within.

As you rest in pure Consciousness, wisdom has room to break through into your personal mind with clarity, perspective, new ideas, helpful ideas, creative ideas, insights, and solutions. These thoughts are what help you gain deeper understanding, keep you from being stuck, and bring all the common sense you need to deal with life's challenges and problems.

This is how wisdom reveals itself to you as a higher quality of thinking. These thoughts are what help you to understand life and others. As you realize more deeply that wisdom is always here waiting to break through, you can trust in wisdom's responsive presence.

Just as the sun brings warmth and nourishment, Mind brings love and wisdom so that your life can move in a healthy direction and you can thrive.

Filling with Mind's love and wisdom aligns you with the intelligence behind life and brings you into greater harmony.

Part 5:
The Principles in daily life

In this section you will see some of the typical questions that we have been asked over the years by our clients and in the seminars that we teach.

Our answers to these questions are not meant to be *your* answers, but they present an opportunity for you to reflect on these questions and to find your own answers from within. We always encourage you to trust in your own wisdom.

We hope these questions and answers will be helpful to you, and will make your experience of the Principles become even more alive and practical.

Try listening with an open mind to discover something lying beyond the beliefs you now possess. You have to remember that you are looking for the unknown, not the known, for original thought.

The Enlightened Gardener
— Sydney Banks

I have been waiting for insights, but I haven't had any. I see other people having insights, when am I going to have mine?

There is no need for you to wait for insights. Wisdom is already breaking through into your consciousness, guiding you and bringing you deeper feelings and helpful thinking. Although this happens on a regular basis, perhaps you don't recognize it. So a good starting point is to begin to look at the ordinary ways that wisdom is already operating in your life.

The more you wake up to Thought, the more space is created in your thinking which allows you to fill with feelings of well-being. Wisdom reveals itself to you and guides you while you are in these feelings. When you fill with well-being you shift in how you see the world, you have a new "sight from within." This is often how insights occur; they are often just a shift in feeling or perspective. A shift might bring you greater clarity, perspective, common sense, and compassion.

The essence of all insight is a shift in consciousness, a shift in how you see and experience the world. At some point there may be words or ideas that follow this shift, but not necessarily.

A shift in consciousness is not only a shift in experience but is a shift in how you know the world. It is a shift from knowing through the intellect, to a higher level of knowing that is more intuitive. You just know what to do without the need for the intellect to first weigh in.

These shifts arise naturally and automatically. You have probably had insights like this today, without even noticing. For instance, you might suddenly remember to call a friend you haven't talked to for a while. Or perhaps you might have been upset with somebody, and then suddenly you have a shift in perception and become more understanding of the person. Having insights is often so ordinary that you don't realize you just had an insight!

Wisdom is not learned, it is unfolded within one's own consciousness. When such knowledge appears to a person, it is revealed in a form that some may call an insight.

The Missing Link: Reflections on Philosophy and Spirit
— Sydney Banks

Can I keep myself from getting caught up in my thinking?

Even as your understanding deepens, you will still get caught up at times. Everyone does. The difference is that with understanding you become more comfortable with being caught up. You just get better at being relaxed about it, and waiting until your thought storm goes away. You continue to have more trust that it will go away and that wisdom will break through. You don't have to do anything!

There begins to be a certainty that it will go away, a certainty that you already have well-being built into you, and a certainty that a single thought or change in perception can change how you feel. The more you realize that you already have within you what you are looking for, the more you can relax into yourself just the way you are, even if you are caught up. It is so helpful when your feelings keep reminding you of the truth of the Principle of Thought.

> How can we stop negative, unwanted thoughts
> from entering our heads? We can't. They come too
> fast and if you try, you will soon find you are on a fool's
> mission. What you can do, however, is realize that your own
> thoughts have no power of their own, only that
> which you give them. However, if you can see that they are
> only thoughts and you refuse to put life into them,
> they are harmless.
>
> *The Missing Link: Reflections on Philosophy and Spirit*
> — Sydney Banks

What's the difference between thinking and Thought?

Thought is a formless power, and it is the Principle that generates the content of your personal thinking.

It is the Principle that creates your thoughts of worry, sadness, contempt, glee, or delight. In a very ordinary way, the Principle of Thought is constantly generating your experiences throughout the day.

How fortunate that as a thinker you are free to use the power of Thought. When you use Thought wisely you realize, as Syd said, that "your thoughts have no power on their own, only that which you give them." This means that thoughts of worry, sadness, or unhappiness have no meaning of their own unless we give them meaning. Any thoughts that have no meaning come and go freely without influencing you adversely. It is like what would happen if your personal thoughts were suddenly in a foreign language that you didn't understand.

If you only pay attention to your thinking you will be endlessly examining the content of your thoughts. Realizing the Principle of Thought allows you to wake up out of the content of your thinking and realize the true source of your experience. This realization will help you. It allows you to stop blaming anything other than Thought for your experience. It allows you to see the temporary, ever-changing, illusory nature of what you feel and see. It allows you to know that what you think is not reality as it is, but is only a fabricated version of reality. And it frees you from the limitations of your personal concepts, ideas, and beliefs.

It's the most natural thing in the world to lose sight of the principle of Thought. It is easy to get lost. To find your way back, you need to see the connection between Thought and thinking.

… they heard something regarding their thoughts —
not through analyzing their thoughts,
but by seeing the power of Thought itself.

The Enlightened Gardener
— Sydney Banks

I don't like when I don't feel good. What can I do about it?

There is nothing wrong with not feeling good. All feelings are friendly and useful. If you were about to step blindly into traffic, and a friend said, "Watch out!", then grabbed your arm and pulled you back onto the curb, you would thank them for keeping you from getting hurt. In the same way, your unpleasant feelings are not "negative." They invite you to just relax and allow wisdom to break through with something new and fresh.

Feelings are just passing thoughts. You can't prevent thoughts from coming into your head. When you see your feelings as friendly and useful, you can use them as a guiding system that opens your mind to new thinking. So you don't have to do anything when you don't feel good. Left to their own devices, feelings change naturally anyway. Understanding the nature of feelings will help you to become accepting of all your feelings.

> All feelings derive and become alive, whether negative or positive, from the power of Thought.
>
> *The Missing Link: Reflections on Philosophy and Spirit*
> — Sydney Banks

I still find myself being reactive to things people say or do. Can you help me with this?

It might appear as if it is a situation or a person outside of yourself that is creating your feelings. But it is how you use the Principle of Thought that determines your feelings moment to moment. When your thinking changes, your feelings change.

When you believe it is the outside world that is making you react, it will make it difficult for you to see that it is completely Thought created. When you wake up to the fact that your reactions are always created from your own thinking it makes it easier to realize the true source of your feelings.

Having reactions is a natural part of human experience. Realizing the true source of your feelings makes it easier for any reaction to come and go more gracefully.

You must look within. And if you look in the personal mind and all the past problems, you are looking outside. You are looking at the mistake. You are looking at the mess. You are looking at the illusion.

"The Consciousness Within"
—Sydney Banks

I often set goals for myself, and then get frustrated when I don't reach them. What can I do about this?

Goals are thoughts that you have made up. In and of themselves, these thoughts are not a problem. It's when you become wedded to your goals, as with any other thoughts, that you innocently close yourself off to new thinking and the ongoing guidance of your wisdom.

When you are attached to outcomes, you are giving your attention to the world of form. When you give your attention to form, you lose sight of your spiritual nature.

When you wake up to the spiritual dimension of life, you open back up to possibilities. You let go of your thinking about objects and you stop being attached to outcomes.

When you let go of your conceptual thinking, wisdom arises as new thinking. It is new thinking that helps you make course corrections in your goals and helps you continue to thrive.

Only in the quiet chambers of your mind will you find real knowledge, for it is here, with the assistance of Mind, Consciousness, and Thought, that the incubation takes place and the wisdom you seek is brought forth into this world of form.

The Enlightened Gardener
— Sydney Banks

I read that Syd Banks said: "Look in the right direction and then do nothing." Does that mean that I don't do anything?

Let's consider for a moment what it means to look in the right direction. This means looking toward the true source of your experience. When you look in this direction your mind naturally quiets down. Your intellect can rest. There is nothing for it to do.

Doing nothing is allowing your personal thinking to fall away. Then you fill up with deeper feelings and understanding, and this guides you into the world in a proactive way. So, at that point you don't sit around doing nothing. Wisdom brings you into engagement with life, with your children, with your job, with other people, or with your challenges.

Doing nothing does not mean your thinking stops. When your intellect is at rest, wisdom still draws upon anything that is helpful from the intellect. Then wisdom works in harmony with the intellect. One example of this is if you have been unhappy with your job for a while, and you have been thinking about what to do about it. As soon as your mind starts to quiet down, wisdom can break through with a new thought of how you might proceed. Now the intellect can be used to put this new idea in motion, drawing upon all your skill and experience. In this way, wisdom and the intellect make a good team.

> I am suggesting to you, to find such knowledge,
> you should stop looking and just be.
>
> *The Enlightened Gardener Revisited*
> — Sydney Banks

I find myself worrying a lot about my problems. Can you speak to that?

It can be very helpful to see that your worry is just thinking you are having in the moment. It's often hard to see that worry is not connected to other people or problems you might be facing. It is just Thought creating an experience of worry in the moment.

When you are not worrying, it doesn't mean you will stop thinking or caring about your problems or other people. When you are no longer worrying, wisdom brings you more helpful thinking in response to what they are thinking, saying, or doing. By trusting wisdom's ability to bring you new and helpful thinking, you start to think better and to feel better. You are back in harmony with life and your innate well-being.

Look deep inside your soul;
this is where you will find the answer.

The Missing Link: Reflections on Philosophy and Spirit
— Sydney Banks

As my understanding of the Principles deepens, do I become numb so that I don't feel life so directly?

As you deepen your understanding of the Principles, in our experience, the opposite happens. You actually feel life *more* deeply. This is because you are not controlling or judging your feelings. You are not trying to exclude any experience from your life. You are free. Understanding the nature of feelings allows them to be what they are. You do less and less thinking about your feelings, and you relax into a state that allows experience to come and go more freely.

You don't become numb. You still feel all of your feelings. But you can allow any feelings without being afraid of them.

With deeper understanding, you become more comfortable in your own skin no matter what you are experiencing. You become more comfortable even when you feel uncomfortable.

Have faith in yourself and know that somewhere deep inside, beyond your ego, beyond your personal self, lies a beautiful flower waiting to unfold. And it is the light of true knowledge that will make it blossom.

The Enlightened Gardener Revisited
— Sydney Banks

What is the cause of addictions, and do the three Principles offer a cure?

It is not uncommon for people to be chronically thinking about things. When this thinking creates an uncomfortable tension, at a certain point the person might start looking for something that they think will bring them relief.

People usually become addicted to drugs, alcohol, sex, gambling, or buying things in an attempt to release the tension and feel better. It is logical that if you think these things are the reason you feel better, you would want more and more of those things.

As people learn about the nature of the principles, they begin to discover how any feeling is created from Thought. When they realize the inside out nature of their experience they stop looking at the outside for their relief and begin to recognize how it is created from within.

When this realization becomes more familiar to people, they no longer need to "self-medicate" to get relief. They have found the true place from which well-being arises.

With understanding, tension doesn't become chronic. This makes it easier for addictions to fall away. Everyone is capable of being transformed from within.

People can be cured from addiction because addiction is created from a persons misunderstanding about where feelings come from. Understanding guides people toward their inner well being. There are no unhealthy side effects or consequences of tapping into one's own well-being. This is more desirable than anything they could find on the outside for temporary relief.

When people realize that there is something within them that they can turn toward and trust, they discover that which truly brings about cure.

When found, wisdom cleanses the channels of the mind and acts like a penicillin for the soul.

The Enlightened Gardener Revisited
— Sydney Banks

Syd Banks has said that what you are looking for is "a state of no-thought." What do you think he was pointing us toward?

Your mind is in a state of no-thought when your mind is free of the influence of your conceptual thinking. It doesn't mean that you do not have thoughts going through your mind. It means that you are not paying attention to, or giving meaning to, your thought content. Specific thoughts are like birds passing through the sky. The sky is not concerned with birds passing through. It allows any bird to fly through.

In a state of no-thought you are just resting in the wide-open field of awareness without concern for the thoughts passing through. This is very different from trying to change your thoughts, improve them, or stop them.

In this state, you experience an enormous freedom from the influence of your conditioned thinking. There is a sense of ease and contentment and the experience of allowing anything to arise. This is peaceful, pleasurable, and rejuvenating.

These feelings are natural and ordinary by-products of being in this state. Syd referred to this state as pure consciousness, silence, the now, or a state of no thought from the intellect.

The state of no-thought is when the personal thought system finds perfect stillness, transcending time, space, and matter, and finds the true nature of Mind.

The Enlightened Gardener Revisited
— Sydney Banks

What does "look within" mean?

When anyone looks at nature and experiences its beauty they are not using a technique. Looking within is not a technique either. It is simply looking in a different direction than we usually do.

"Within" is the space within consciousness that is before any thinking content such as your thoughts, ideas, beliefs, or concepts. It is before any thought you can hear in your head. "Within" is that which is prior to the formation of your experience. Sometimes this dimension is called the unknown.

"Looking" is recognizing or sensing or resting in what lies before your personal thinking, or the thinking that you do.

"Looking within" is touching upon that quiet space within where wisdom can break through into human consciousness.

To look within is to sense your inner space. It is a vast, quiet space. This looking is a wide-open awareness that does not focus on any content of experience. This awareness does not concentrate on the content of a thought or listen to its message, for example. It does not give it meaning. You are looking at Thought, which is the formless energy that gives rise to all of your thinking forms. What arises in that space are thoughts that you can see or hear, ideas, images, perceptions, sensations, feelings, emotions.

But to find the answer you must turn around and
look inside. And you step inside, inside to your very soul.
Now remember, your soul is consciousness. Step into that
divine consciousness that lies within and there you
will find the answer.

"The Consciousness Within"
— Sydney Banks

I once heard Syd Banks say, "Just be ordinary." I'm not sure I want to just be ordinary. Can you speak to this?

A lot of people equate being ordinary with being boring; they're afraid people won't be interested in someone who is ordinary. But what is meant by "just be ordinary" is to be comfortable being yourself, just as you are. Being comfortable in your own skin. The paradox is that when you are comfortable with yourself just as you are, your mind is most receptive to wisdom. It is wisdom that allows you to be authentic, creative, and lighthearted. Actually, it is more likely that people will like you when you are comfortable with yourself just as you are.

Trying to be special, different, or better requires a lot of effort and thinking. It is based on dissatisfaction with your self, and such effortful thinking now adds stress to your dissatisfaction. Realizing the Principles allows you to accept the perfection of how you are at each moment.

> Try to be content with what you have and it may
> surprise you how the quality of your life could change.
> Contentment is a state of being that always comes
> clothed in a positive feeling. Contentment brings peace
> of mind and happiness into one's life.
>
> *The Enlightened Gardener Revisited*
> — Sydney Banks

I am struggling with a big decision and no matter how much I think about it, I don't know what to do. What am I doing wrong?

When you say that you are struggling, it can be good to realize that struggle is an experience created from Thought. When you are caught up in thoughts of struggle, it will be hard for you to get new thinking. When you are trying to make a decision, what you are looking for is new thinking. It may seem strange at first, but the more you think about your decision in a way that creates struggle, the further away you will be from a solution.

When you realize that you can't think your way to new thinking, you begin to look in the direction of a quiet, open, and reflective mind. This creates the space necessary for new thinking to arise. It is from this space that decisions are made.

When your mind is still enough and goes into the state of no personal thought, the incubation takes place and the wisdom you seek will be brought to life.

The Enlightened Gardener Revisited
— Sydney Banks

**If understanding the Principles helps me
to get over my painful feelings more quickly,
am I then denying those feelings?**

If you are holding onto a really hot pan and you are being burned, you are not denying your feeling of pain if you immediately drop the hot pan. It is natural for human beings to let go of what is painful.

When painful feelings pass naturally, it is not denial. The ability to get over painful feelings is called resilience and is a characteristic of healthy functioning. It is wisdom that moves you in a healthy direction.

I do not ask anyone to ignore their past experiences.
This would be denial, and denial is not a healthy state.
Instead, seek a clearer understanding of the past; realize
that the negative feelings and emotions from past traumatic
experiences are no longer true. They are merely memories,
a collection of old, stale thoughts.

The Missing Link: Reflections on Philosophy and Spirit
— Sydney Banks

As a student of the Principles, do you still meditate?

Not in the traditional sense. Often people see meditation as a practice to be done. They think of it as sitting in a certain posture, for a certain length of time, following someone else's instructions for how to do the meditation.

Meditation is the natural state of mind that reveals itself when your head is free of personal thinking. It is free of the influence of your ideas, beliefs, and concepts.

Realizing the Principles leads you to this natural meditative state. When you wake up to the fact of Thought, you stop being influenced by your personal thinking and you rest in the now.

The now is a wide-open awareness when you are no longer caught up in any of the thoughts going through your mind. You are fully present, relaxed and alert. This is your natural meditative state. At some point during the day everyone spontaneously falls into this natural meditative state.

Therefore, the meditative state is your natural state. It is always there but is covered over by your involvement in personal thinking. Meditation is not something you arrive at as a result of doing something. It is the essence of who you are.

There is no fixed way to get oneself into the state of meditation. The state of meditation comes when the ego is put to sleep via silence.

Second Chance
— Sydney Banks

What is free will?

Just because a thought comes into your head doesn't mean you have to focus your attention on it and continue to think about it. Our free will allows us to take our attention off of what we are thinking about.

Free will is like the steering wheel on a car. For example, if you are driving down the road and there is a big pothole in front of you, it makes sense to steer around it. You wouldn't think you needed to go into it just to experience it. Using your free will allows your mind to open to new thinking. It doesn't mean you are denying what you were experiencing. When you take attention off of what you are thinking, your mind opens up to new thinking.

At any given time, you can choose to open to the new. There are billions of different thoughts you can have at any moment and it's your choice which one to pay attention to. What you choose to pay attention to will create an experience in you. If that experience is a painful feeling, you can choose to take your attention off of what you are focused on and then be open to the limitless capacity of the Mind to bring fresh and helpful thinking.

Among the greatest gifts given to us are
the powers of free thought and free will, which give us
the stamp of individuality...

The Missing Link: Reflections on Philosophy and Spirit
— Sydney Banks

How do I know if my intuition is coming from wisdom, and not from my ego?

Intuition that comes from wisdom has a certain feeling to it. Intuition arises naturally when our minds are clear and we are not engaged in our personal thinking. It comes fresh and it often has an element of surprise to it. The quality of the feeling lacks tension and is positive. When wisdom breaks through, it will naturally move you into action.

The quality of your feeling is one way of knowing if it is wisdom moving you to action or if it is ego. When your thoughts quiet down, and you start to feel better, that's the feeling that you are looking for. When it is ego, it often feels like excitement and your thinking starts to race with all of the things that you think you should be doing. It's a high-energy feeling, as opposed to the calm, quiet knowing that occurs when wisdom moves you in a direction.

You can learn to become more and more sensitive to the lightness-feeling quality that is the indicator whether you can trust that thinking. Wisdom can arise at any time. It is an uplifting feeling that arises naturally when your mind is quiet. Trusting this feeling allows you to make decisions based on your wisdom instead of your ego.

Wisdom is not found in the world of form,
nor in remote corners of the globe. Wisdom lies within
our own consciousness.

The Missing Link: Reflections on Philosophy and Spirit
— Sydney Banks

Part 6:
Living a life aligned with love and wisdom

The more you realize the nature of the Principles, the more you replicate nature. You align yourself with the nature of life itself, which is free, full of potential, creative, and giving. You replicate the creative process of the universe itself, and that's where your greatest freedom lies.

As your understanding of the Principles deepens, you stop thinking about yourself so much, and just go about living your life. When you are less self-conscious you live more fully engaged in the present as love and wisdom move you beautifully and gracefully through life.

Life is a divine mystery and once you realize that,
you join the mystery … Divine Mind is pure love. Divine
Consciousness is pure love. Divine Thought is pure love.
It's a different kind of love. It's nothing to do with this
physical world — you're in love with the world.

"The Hawaii Lecture Series"
— Sydney Banks

Wisdom is an inborn spiritual knowledge that
lies deep within the soul of all human beings.
Wisdom is revealed from the inside-out.

The Enlightened Gardener
— Sydney Banks

Love

There are many different ways of talking about love. Usually, when people talk about love, they only point toward the human psychological feeling of love.

Another way of talking about love is by pointing to the unconditionally generous nature of life. The formless, or spiritual, nature of life is constantly and unconditionally giving of itself so that life can exist. Right now, as you read this, life is bursting forth as you and everything else that you experience. You have the ability to live fully and generously in each moment.

Generosity of spirit is love.

Your true nature is identical with the source of life. It is generating and giving unconditionally. All that you see has been created from the same source. It is out of the generosity of spirit that everything that exists is created.

If the nature of life is to give unconditionally and generously it would make sense that, as you align yourself with this source, you too will become more unconditionally giving and generous. You become kinder, gentler, more loving as you align with your true nature.

Love is the very nature of life. It is your very nature to love. It's built into the very fabric of life for you to be unconditionally generous and giving. It's only when you get caught up in your thinking that you lose sight of that which is invisibly living you. When you lose sight of your true nature you tend to be less kind, less loving, more egocentric. You feel separate from life and stop giving freely and unconditionally. It is nice to realize that this is not your true nature.

You are already hard-wired for love.

Wisdom

Wisdom is an intelligence that transcends the personal. The problem is we personalize wisdom. We think it is my wisdom. We think we have to access it or tap into it. In fact, wisdom works beautifully without our interference. It guides us toward thriving in the same way it does for everything in nature.

Wisdom is not operated by the intellect.
It operates the intellect!

When your personal thinking quiets down, wisdom can operate most effectively and efficiently. Then wisdom guides you effortlessly through your life. It is always there trying to break through but it is hard to hear your wisdom when you are caught up in, and listening to, your insecure thinking.

Wisdom brings you answers to your problems. Wisdom knows how to bring you thoughts and feelings best suited for who you are and the situation you are in. When you are being guided by wisdom, you just know what to do and when to do it. The right feelings and words show up spontaneously. Decisions come to mind effortlessly. Healthy behavior happens. You just intuitively know what to do. You naturally find yourself being kind and loving.

As you begin to live a life aligned with wisdom you begin to see how wisdom underlies all of life, and you begin to get a glimpse of the unity of life. You become loving, understanding, and compassionate toward the full range of human experience.

Trusting wisdom allows for a surrender of any thought that limits your love and understanding. There comes a freedom as you stop running from suffering, and understand the nature of any experience. You are at ease with who and what you are. You naturally experience compassion for the pain and suffering in yourself and other people. Wisdom helps you respond to this suffering in a way that is helpful.

Wisdom is built into the very nature of our being and therefore it is built into us to move in a healthy direction.

Freeing the light within

In your natural state you are like a lighthouse. This becomes obvious when we look at children before they start to get caught up in personal thinking. Fortunately, this light is within you. It is innate, which means that you are born with this divine spark.

Because you are born into the world of form you often lose sight of this inner spark of light. When you are constantly looking at the physical world, all you see is form and it becomes easy to forget the light that is the essence of your nature. Your spiritual nature is always present; it's the source and foundation of all of life.

Realizing your spiritual nature frees your inner light and allows it to shine through into every part of your life.

It seems as if we keep forgetting what our true essence is. We all have divine light underneath the chatter of our personal thought system, and whenever we touch this quiet space it invokes feelings of love and connection.

Here, light is being used as a metaphor for universal love and wisdom. This love and wisdom does not originate from your conceptual mind. It embraces everything, just like the light of the sun embraces everything indiscriminately.

One of the oldest metaphors for human psychological functioning is the metaphor of clouds, sky, and sun. Your thoughts and feelings are like the clouds, consciousness is like the sky, and love and wisdom are like the light of the sun.

You can't think your way to well-being. It is not a matter of trying to think better and feel better. Effort and trying are thoughts that create a degree of stress. Stress clouds over the light of your love and wisdom.

Like the weather, when the sky is clouded over it covers the sun. When the clouds are dark and stormy not much sunlight gets through. Sunlight provides warmth and nourishment and is necessary for life to grow and thrive.

When the clouds of your personal thinking fall away, the light of love and wisdom is ready to shine through. Your light shines until the moment when you again get caught up in your personal thinking and these thought clouds obstruct your light.

It's easy to see whether a person's light is shining through their eyes or not. As a person's thinking clears, their inner light comes pouring out through their eyes again. Sometimes we speak of people as having "a light in their eyes," and we also say that the eyes are the windows to the soul.

When your inner light shines through it brings warmth and nourishment. It brings feelings of well-being and thoughts that are helpful.

The more your inner light shines through, the more you become light-hearted, kind, gentle, comfortable, and loving.

The dance and celebration of life

There is an incredible dance going on, that has always been going on, and always will go on.

Out of nothing everything dances into existence.

It's like music: there is a field of silence, and then a musical note appears. And then another one, and then sometimes you get beautiful pieces of music. From this infinite field of nothingness there is a movement of energy that dances into form. There is silence, and then something appears within the silence.

In music, there are only so many notes, and yet look at how many songs have been made through the years from the same limited number of notes.

You have a unique song to play. The more trust you have in wisdom the more you allow your song to be played through and as you.

Even though there are universal characteristics of well-being, wisdom blends in those notes to create your unique song.

It's a paradox that you have to go beyond the personal to discover the uniqueness of your song.

The beauty of life, the mystery of life, is that anything can dance into existence. The Principles are creative forces that generate all of life. They allow you to have experiences and be aware of both form and formless.

We talk about three Principles, but they are really aspects of one Principle. It is a movement from nothing into something. It's the movement from pure energy into form.

Everything is the same dance of energy
whether in form or formless.

A deeper understanding of the Principles will make it easier for you to celebrate what it means to be a human being. It allows you to enjoy your participation in this dance we call life.

Why do you, along with so many of us, at times lose the enjoyment of this dance? When you are born, you quickly forget the formless, spiritual part of your being and become more and more identified with only the human part, the ego.

If you look back on your life you can have a sense that who you are has always existed. You sense that what you call "you" was always there having all of the thoughts, feelings, and experiences that you had. Your being has always been here throughout your life. Your thoughts, feelings, and perceptions dance into and out of existence. But at any moment you can sense your existence.

In essence, who you are is the awareness
of the dance.

Just like you never forget your name, on some level you never forget who you really are. It's just been covered over by a simple misunderstanding. Innocently you forget your true essence of being.

You see how you are one with the
dance of life and can celebrate the beauty
and mystery of this dance.

Bringing more love and wisdom into the world

Bringing more love and wisdom into the world is an ordinary process that is available to you and everyone else at any given moment.

A deeper understanding of the Principles shows up as generosity of spirit and service to others. With more understanding you naturally begin to be kinder and more compassionate toward yourself and others, even during those times when you are not feeling good.

The light of understanding illuminates the true nature of life. When your inner light shines through, you bring that light into the world. This is a way you can be of service to people. The feelings that you bring to others really matter, so letting your light shine through is a wonderful way you can impact the people around you. It becomes easier to be fully present to others and really listen, to appreciate them for who they are and to bring them compassion and loving-kindness.

Anytime you go inside and bring more presence, warmth, kindness, and deeper listening into the world, you are literally helping to change the world. If you see Consciousness as a universal eco-system, then any time you improve a part of that system, everyone in that system will be positively affected. When you bring more love and understanding to the world, you are helping your family, friends, community, and ultimately the world to thrive. You are literally helping to raise the overall level of understanding of the world.

Just by increasing your level of understanding, you will bring more love and wisdom into the world.

Part 7:
Realizing the deep quiet of your being

As your understanding of the Principles deepens, you will begin to realize the deep quiet of your inner being.

As you realize that this deep quiet is always within, you will stop using your own efforts to quiet your mind. You will simply become aware of, and rest in, this eternal quiet. As you become familiar with the depth and beauty of this quiet you will naturally be drawn within. And as your realization of the nature of your being deepens further you will stabilize in this natural quiet.

It is out of this quiet that our love and wisdom are free to arise.

We're searching for a silent mind. It's in the silence of the mind that all the secrets of life are found, where all happiness is found. Where the keys are found. And the second you open that door, you find a new level of consciousness. It is a must, life must become more beautiful.

"The Quiet Mind"
— Sydney Banks

A quiet mind

In the quiet of your mind you can go from direct experience to realization of the Principles. Only realization allows you to intuit what lies beyond your experience to where the Principles are found.

At different moments in your life you have experienced your mind becoming quiet and at those times you have felt connected to life. These moments can feel different to each person. You may experience this as a peaceful, all-inclusive, expansive feeling. You might experience it as wonder or mystery. These moments, whether ordinary or profound, have an impact on you. Outside these moments, you and everyone else will often lose sight of the fact that you are already intimately connected to the whole of life.

We are all longing for unity.

Often these moments of connection happen to you spontaneously. The sense of being connected to something greater than yourself is something that you will want to re-experience, but the problem is that most often you will look in the opposite direction to where it is actually found.

You are born into a physical body, and when you open your eyes you see the physical world you are living in. So you start looking in the world to find the sense of wonder and to be connected to something deeper, something greater than yourself. Your search is based on a misunderstanding about what brings about this sense of a quiet mind, wonder, and connectedness.

You, like most people, may start a search for methods or techniques to get back to this sense of peace and connectedness. The problem is that when you are trying to create a quiet mind, you can't help but have a lot of thinking about it. So, while attempting to quiet your mind, you may find that your mind is becoming more and more busy.

It would be like looking at a turbulent ocean and wanting it to be still. If, in an attempt to make it still, you were to start hitting the waves with a tennis racket, it just wouldn't work.

This would be an innocent attempt to find a quiet mind through your own self-efforts. But what if, instead of hitting the ocean with a tennis racket, you stopped worrying about the waves? If you didn't try to control or stop the waves?

What if you simply dropped a foot below the surface and noticed how your experience changed? Below the surface is less turbulence. Then, if you were to drop another foot deeper, and another foot deeper, it would become even quieter. If you went deep enough you would find stillness.

What is helpful is to recognize that the quiet and the stillness is always here. So, it makes a difference whether your mind is turbulent and you think it should be quiet, or if you think there is a quiet that is always present. What a difference if you realize that you already have what you are looking for; that this is not something you can, or need to, make happen through your own efforts.

Once you begin to realize that you already have what you are looking for without trying, you can begin to relax into that space. It's like falling asleep. You fall into this quiet that is already there within you.

You, like all of us, can touch that space. You have the capacity to discover or realize, through insight, your true nature because it's already there within you.

Your true nature is the here that is always there.

All that is required to discover this silent mind is a very subtle shift in attention away from the waves and the turbulence, away from the things of the world, and toward the space that is always there — quiet, welcoming, present, waiting. It's the only thing you can't get to by trying. And the instant you realize that truth and stop trying, you are able to experience your natural state of mind.

This natural state is always right there beneath the noise of your babbling thought system. Realizing its presence is not a matter of having to quiet your mind. It's not a doing. It's about realizing what is already here.

Anyone trying to help you realize this presence or space can only use words that point you to look in that direction, hoping by doing so that you may first experience and then realize what lies within. But this is an inner space before your thinking. It is untouched by life, and it's unspoiled by words. It's before any words. It is the now. Not the now in time, but the now before time, before any concept of time that we may have. It is your soul. It's pure awareness. It's an inner sky — a sky that holds nothing, clings to nothing. It's your core, your essence.

Sydney Banks said that when you touch or glimpse that space "it's a must, life must become more beautiful." Something beautiful must manifest through you.

You may experience a contented peace, a warmth spreading through you, a sense of opening, a relaxing, a sense of aliveness, a clarity, or a new thought. You may experience unconditional happiness, joy, or love.

As soon as you start thinking about it, you will lose it. As soon as you try to make it stay, you will lose it. Maintaining that space is not a matter of figuring out what you are thinking or feeling, because that brings you right back to your conceptual mind. You can't find it by using your conceptual mind; it would be impossible because this space lies before or beyond your conceptual mind.

This inner space is the always-present backdrop within which all thoughts come and go.

This is your birthright. You are already immersed in this vast, magnificent, silent awareness. Just listen. When you really listen, your personal thinking falls away. Listen until a feeling begins to fill you. It's very subtle. It's very simple. It's what everyone is looking for.

This space is all welcoming like the sky. The sky doesn't say *this* bird is welcome to fly through and *that* bird is not welcome to fly through. This cloud is okay but not that cloud. I am not having any lightning here. The sky doesn't judge or select what may or may not be in its space. The sky is all-welcoming.

When you fall into this non-conceptual space there may still be concepts, ideas, and thoughts that come through, but you are not giving your attention to them. You don't cling to them. They just pass through like birds in the sky. Thoughts come and go but the space doesn't come and go. The silence doesn't come and go. Everything arises out of that space and is made from that same energy.

Waves are not a problem for the ocean. The ocean is not trying to quiet down its waves. You may have an idea about what quiet looks like and then try to accomplish it through your own efforts. People have innocently been doing that for centuries. But in nature, waves and thunderstorms don't need quieting.

When you rest in the space before your ideas and concepts, thunderstorms can come and go but the thunderstorm doesn't define who you are.

Whatever you think you are, you are not.

As you rest in this space you can intuit that it doesn't come and go. It's your true self. It's your very being. Your ideas of who you are come and go in that space, but they are not who you are. This is not something that you can understand intellectually but all of us can experience it and realize the truth of it.

A quiet mind cannot be found by your intellect.

When you rest in the now, thoughts come and go, feelings come and go. Beneath all that comes and goes is a peace that is always here, always present. The more you touch this space, the more it embraces all of your life. It doesn't discriminate, it doesn't judge, it doesn't select. It doesn't say this feeling is okay, that one isn't, this thought is okay but that one isn't. You become more sky-like in nature. You become more aligned with inner being, your true self. It's very freeing.

You are always connected to the Principles, to the spiritual nature of life, to the infinite field of energy in which you participate and dance. If you are connected to this field, then you are connected intimately and directly to the intelligence of all things. When the intelligence of all things breaks through into your consciousness it is wisdom breaking through into your mind as clarity, perspective, common sense, good ideas, love, and connection. It's what unravels your egocentric view of yourself and others. It's what will bring you what you are looking for.

When you don't understand that everything comes from within, you will inevitably believe that your feelings are connected to something on the outside rather than being created from within. This misunderstanding has created so much suffering through the ages.

Nothing that has already been created has the power to create.

Nothing on the outside of you can make you feel a certain way. Only that which has the power to create can create.

You can discover for yourself this secret that many wise people throughout the ages have done their best to tell. It's not a secret because it's a secret, it's a secret because anything said about it is not it!

Part 8:
Coming home

Within you there is another world. When you become immersed in this inner space, you will never come to the end of what can be revealed to you. That which is revealed to you will be uplifting and nourishing. As you become more intimately familiar with this space you also will intuit the loving and wise nature of your inner being. Coming home is waking up to this always-existing inner world.

Look within. What you are searching for comes from within. You can't find what you are looking for in the external world.

As you look within, wisdom breaks through into the world, guiding and directing you home. Then at some point, without any effort on your part, you begin to intuit the unity of life.

You realize you have always been home
and have never really left.

We are all searching for our home grounds.
We're searching to find the way home. And to find the way
home, what we have to do is look at everything
in reverse, because naturally if you're away from home,
if you keep walking you walk further away. To find
home you've got to turn around. You have got to go the
opposite direction and instead of searching outside for the
answer you seek, all you do is turn around and look
inside. And there lie the secrets that you want.

"The Best of Two Worlds"
— Sydney Banks

Coming home brings hope

Realizing the Principles brings hope that:

- You already have what you need to wake up out of the illusion of ego-bound thinking and its temporarily created unhappiness.
- You already have within you a space of awareness that is free of the influence of limited, conditioned thinking.
- Whenever you touch this space you will experience love and wisdom.

This hope allows us to celebrate being human. The human part of being human is that we have all kinds of thoughts and feelings and they come and go. That's always going to be true. It's like having all kinds of internal weather. Sometimes the sun shines and sometimes it rains. That is always going to be true.

But often you, like all of us, will forget that you are part of something much greater, that you are at one with the intelligence behind all of life. This intelligence doesn't care that you have different kinds of weather, just like the sky doesn't care if it rains or snows. Weather is just what happens within the sky.

Coming home is resting in a space that embraces all experiences. It's seeing the truth that every single thought you have is neutral and it doesn't mean anything unless you give it significance. It's like looking at the weather and not judging it. It's not like the sun is good, and it shouldn't rain. All kinds of weather are going to be present, and the more you see the impersonal truth of that in terms of your thought content, the more at ease you will be. Having different kinds of weather is part of life.

Coming home is embracing all of your humanity. When you don't fight against yourself you can be more at peace in the midst of all kinds of experiences, including self-doubt, worry, anxiety, and other kinds of internal weather.

When you are resting in the space of being, you attach less meaning to the comings and goings of the weather in your system. It's normal to have weather. Being home is knowing that you are one with something far greater, and it is having faith that the blue sky is always there behind the clouds. The sun and wisdom are always there, ready to shine through as soon as your clouds dissolve.

Coming home is realizing the truth of what it is that is creating all of your experiencing, and then being at ease with all the different experiences that life brings you as a human being. It's not something that you have to believe, it's something that you will begin to see for yourself. We are not trying to convince you of anything, we are simply trying to point you to look in a direction so that you can find truth for yourself.

Realizing your true home

Realizing the richness of the Three Principles reveals your true home.

The depth and beauty of the Three Principles is indescribable. All three Principles point toward a unified richness that can more fully be experienced and known by you as you delve deeply into the experience of each Principle.

The Three Principles together add a fuller sense of possibilities. Each Principle is like a separate musical key that, when brought together, allows innumerable symphonies to be created.

All Three Principles point toward the same vast inner space. This inner space is completely empty, yet gives birth to all that has an existence in the world of form. So it is an emptiness that simultaneously creates the full range of any experience you can or will have in your life.

We would love for you to immerse yourselves experientially into the depths of your inner being even now, as you read this. In a moment of inner stillness and heightened awareness of your own inner being, you may actually be able to sense and intuit this quiet space within. You may be able to notice that all of your thoughts, images, feelings, and sensations arise out of this space. While you are immersed in this space your sense of self may momentarily dissolve.

All that remains is the coming and going of sensory experience. While immersed in this experience you are not thinking about or conceptualizing anything about the Principle of Thought. You are actually experiencing this Principle directly, unmediated by concepts or beliefs. You are simply being. You are standing in awe at the very birthplace of your experiential life.

In a moment of absolute attention to this inner space you may also become aware of your awareness itself. This pure Consciousness is silently aware of all that arises as objects of experience. This awareness is untouched by what it is aware of. It is never damaged or altered by what passes through it, much as the sky is untouched by the birds flying through it.

Being Home

When resting in pure Consciousness, you are able to be aware of the coming and going of any thought and feeling without being identified with it. There is such freedom in having an impersonal relationship with your thinking and feelings. There is freedom in not being identified with the content of your experience. At some moment you may experience that this pure Consciousness is who you really are.

What comes and goes is like clothes you put on and take off. These clothes do not define who you really are. Each thought and feeling can then be experienced neutrally without giving meaning to it. This allows the content of your experience to come and go freely and naturally without grabbing your attention and without you having to feel responsible for what is created. In this way you can directly experience the Principle of Consciousness.

In a moment of silent awareness, you can intuit the very source of creation. There is a feeling of aliveness and a sense of infinite possibilities. There is no sense of a separate self — there is only the existence of oneness. There is a knowing of wisdom and love. This is a glimpse of the Principle of Mind.

As you become more familiar with immersing yourself in this inner space you naturally begin to experience gratitude for the creative nature of Thought, the freedom of pure Consciousness, and the wisdom of Mind.

You may be fortunate enough to realize that this space is your true self, and is always here. We hope that, as you have been reading this book, you have realized this space to be your true home.

Welcome home!

About the authors

Dr. Dicken Bettinger, Ed.D.

I have had a long career as a licensed psychologist and as an educator. My current business is 3 Principles Mentoring, which I founded to guide individuals, groups, and organizations in deepening their understanding of the Three Principles. I lead seminars around the world in the Three Principles as taught by my teacher Mr. Sydney Banks. I met Sydney Banks in 1986 and feel fortunate that, for 23 years, I was able to learn directly from him. My seminars teach the foundations behind mental well-being and point people toward their own wisdom.

In 1991, I co-founded the first Three Principles center in the Northeastern U.S. Later, I spent 16 years as a senior staff associate at Pransky and Associates where I developed and led corporate and university leadership trainings, team development, and executive coaching. I worked with individuals and couples to help them raise their levels of well-being.

I am a graduate of St. Lawrence University, received my Master's Degree from Penn State University, and my Doctorate in Counseling Psychology from Boston University. My wife Coizie and I have been married since 1969 and have two children and two grandchildren. I enjoy photography, hiking, canoeing, and traveling. I am so grateful for this deep understanding that allows me to navigate life with ease and joy.

Natasha Swerdloff

I first came across this understanding in 2012 when a friend told me about something she called The Three Principles. I had not heard about it before, and having been interested in personal growth and integral psychology for 25 years I was a bit skeptical.

I went to my first training — everything I heard sounded so simple and I felt like I already knew what was being talked about. It intuitively made sense to me, so it felt like arriving back home to a space inside that I always knew was there but had forgotten about.

In the beginning, I was looking for the "how to," the "3 magic steps," or some sort of application that would make it easy for me to teach this to others.

I have been self-employed since 1996 and have delivered business trainings and executive coaching and often talk at conferences all over the world, so finding ways of getting this simple message across was of value to me.

It took a while before I realized that this understanding is insight-based, and that there are no "quick fixes" or "how-tos." I now own The Principles Institute and provide organizational development, consulting, training, and coaching with a Three Principles-based approach.

I am based in Denmark, married to John, and enjoy spending time with friends and family, cooking, gardening, being in nature, traveling, and riding my Harley-Davidson in the summer time.

Resources

Dicken and Natasha both lead seminars and speak at conferences all over the world. They each offer mentoring, supervision of practitioners, coaching, and intensives.

You can find more information on their websites

Dicken's website: **www.3principlesmentoring.com**
Natasha's website: **www.theprinciplesinstitute.com**

We highly recommend that you study the works of Sydney Banks directly.

You can find information about his books, videos, and recordings at the following website: **www.sydneybanks.org**

34321078R00072

Printed in Poland
by Amazon Fulfillment
Poland Sp. z o.o., Wrocław